4/10

D0475408

THE SMASH! SMASH! TRUCK

By Professor Potts

For
Quentin, Arthur
and Johnny Rotten

A man that looks on glass,
On it may stay his eye;
Or, if he pleaseth, through
it pass,
And then the heav'n espy.
— George Herbert,
'The Elixir' (1633)

d|b
FICKLING
David Fickling Books

Most scientists believe recycling began 14 billion years ago, when our universe was created.

Absolutely EVERYTHING we see and touch — me, you and glass bottles too — started with a FANTASTIC loudest-ever sound: the

BIG BANG

Very, very tiny bits of matter called atoms were created.

We could see atoms if we made things a billion times bigger.

The smallest dot on this page may contain 10 million atoms.

All things are made of atoms.

Atoms don't wear out.

They move around, sticking together . . .

. . . and coming apart.

Atoms swirled together to form the Earth 4.5 billion years ago.

Since then very little has been added
and almost nothing taken away.
It is a constantly changing
merry-go-round.

The Earth recycles atoms.

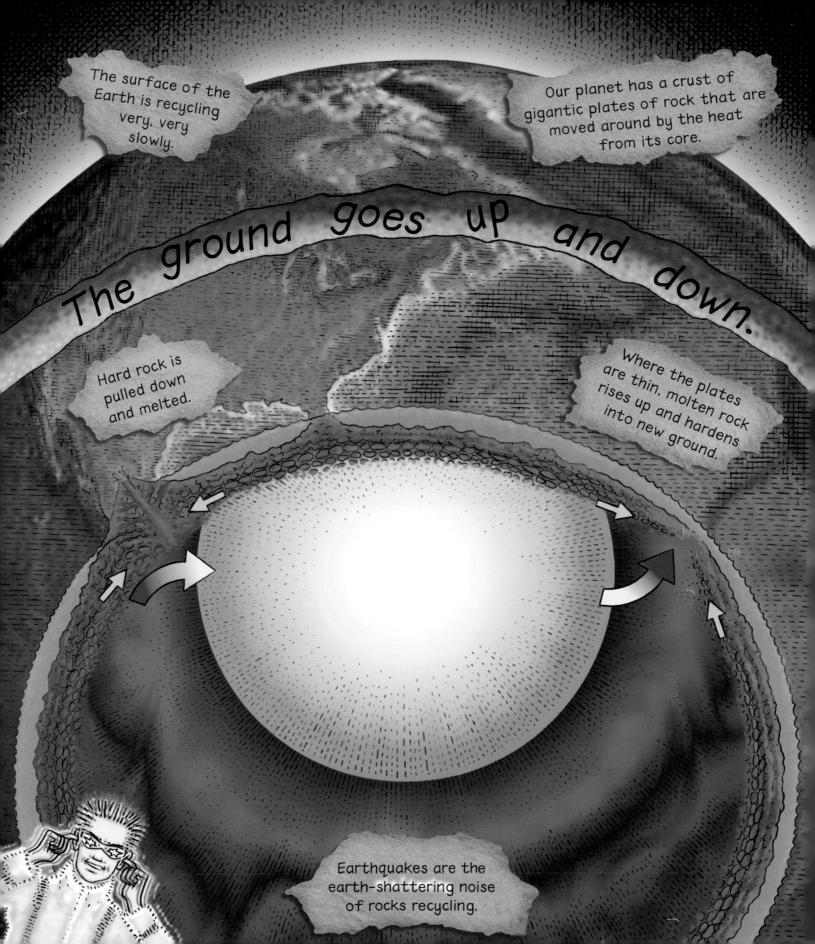

The
Sun sends
water round
and round.

Every second
seas and lakes are
heated by the Sun.
Water turns into steam,
which rises into the sky.
It gathers into clouds and
falls down to Earth as rain.
Rain that falls on land
runs into lakes
and seas.

Plants grow
by using atoms from the
air and ground. They
breathe out atoms. When
they die, they decompose.
Their atoms are scattered
and reused.

Plant Cycle

It's our turn.

All
living
creatures
are made by
recycling the
Earth's atoms.

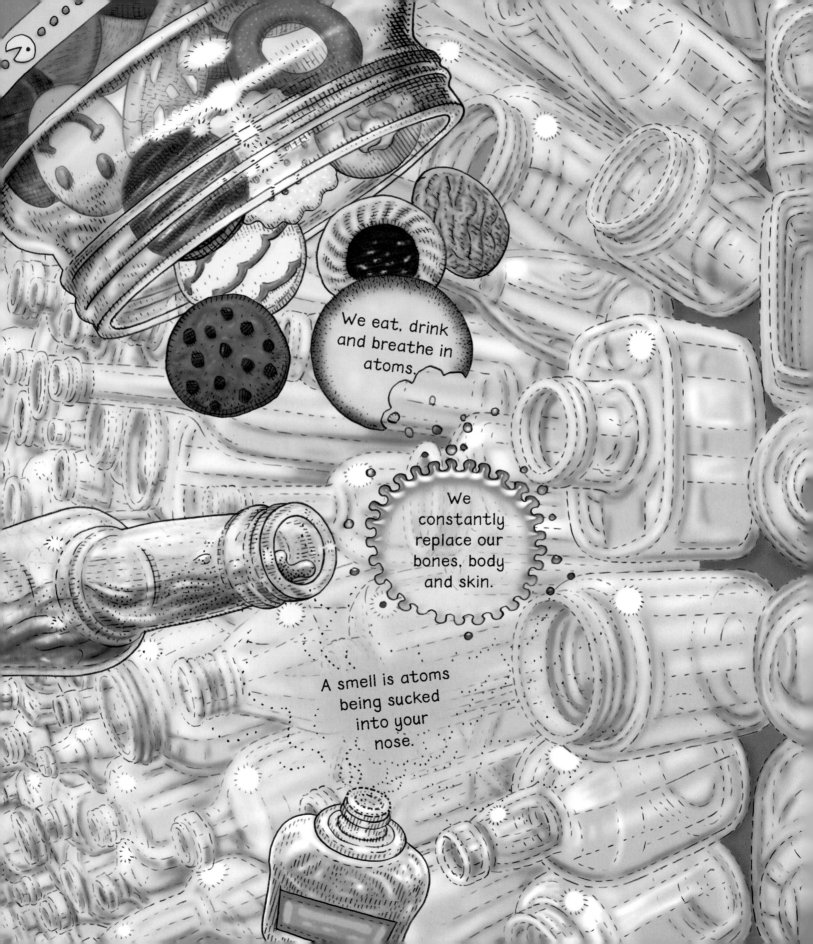

Unsmashed glass in a trash dump will eventually become part of something else.

But glass is so hard that it will take HUNDREDS OF THOUSANDS OF YEARS to smash up.

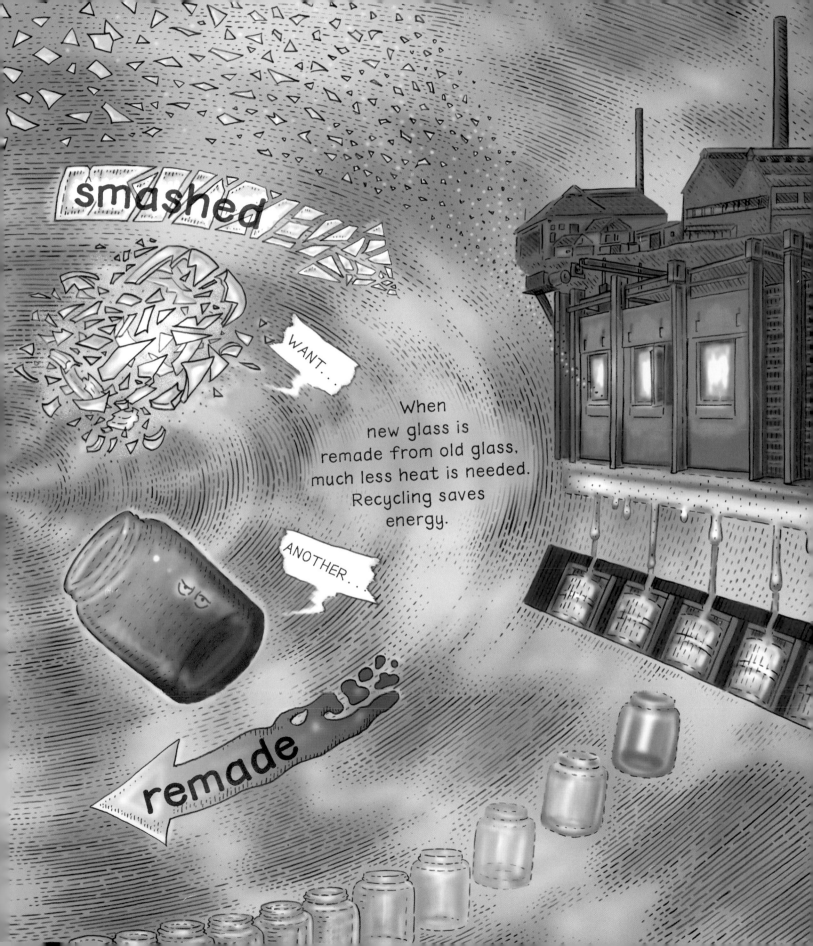

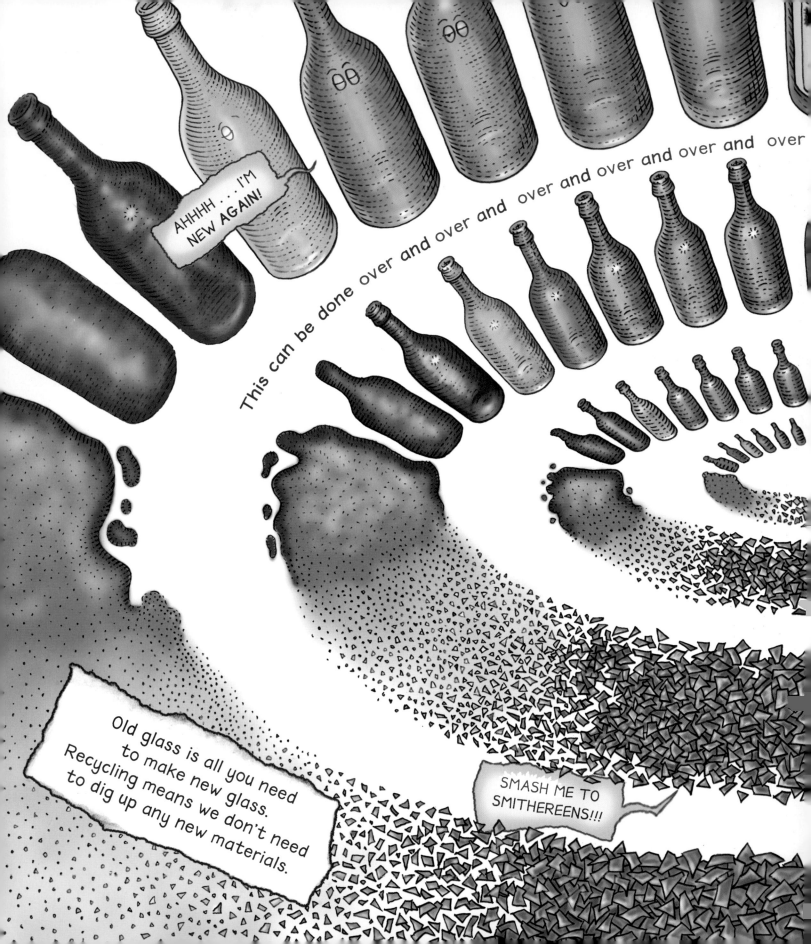

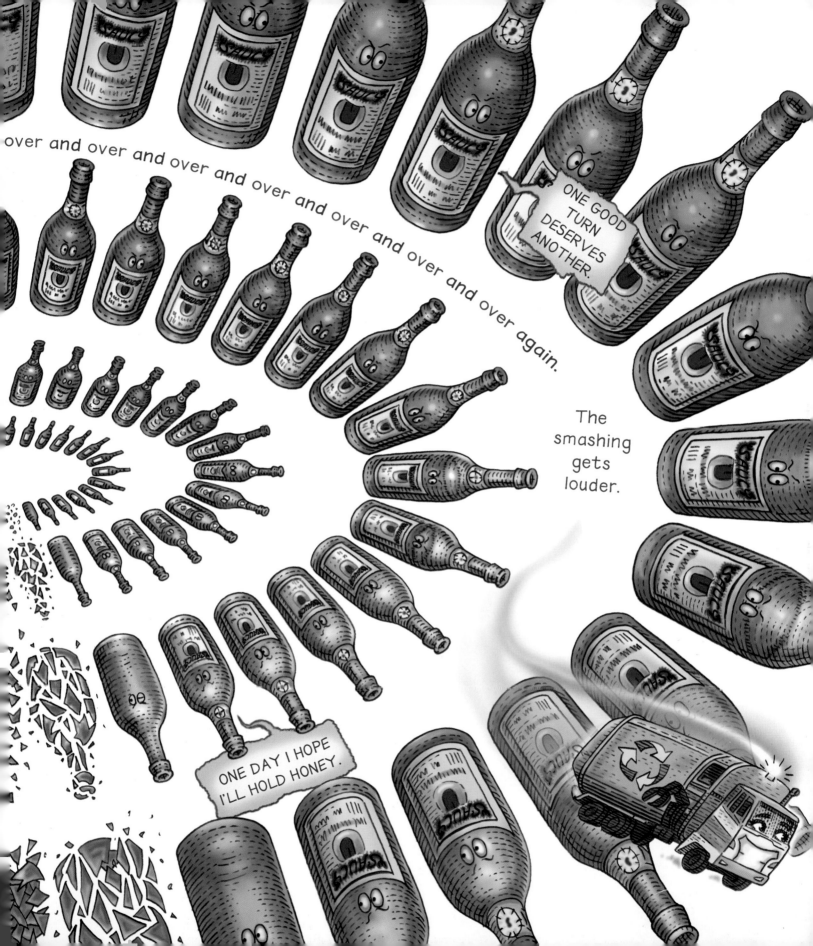

Emptying the truck at the recycling depot makes a giant SMASH!

There's a louder SMASH when the container trucks are loaded.

It's loudest
when the
trucks unload
at the glass
factory.

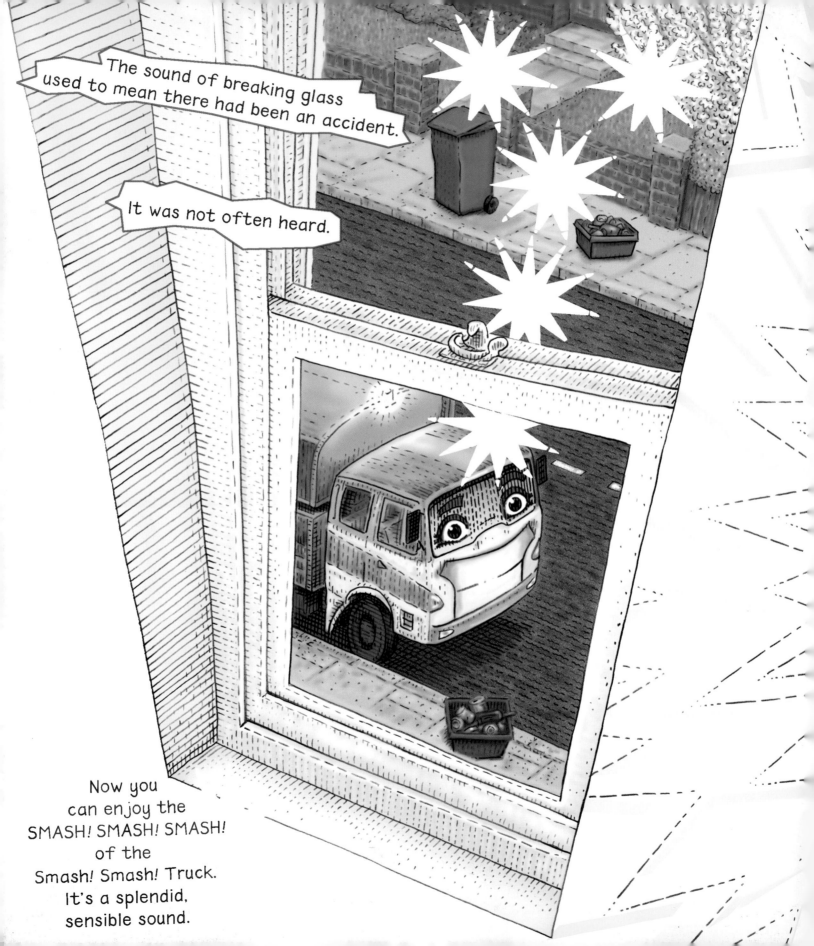

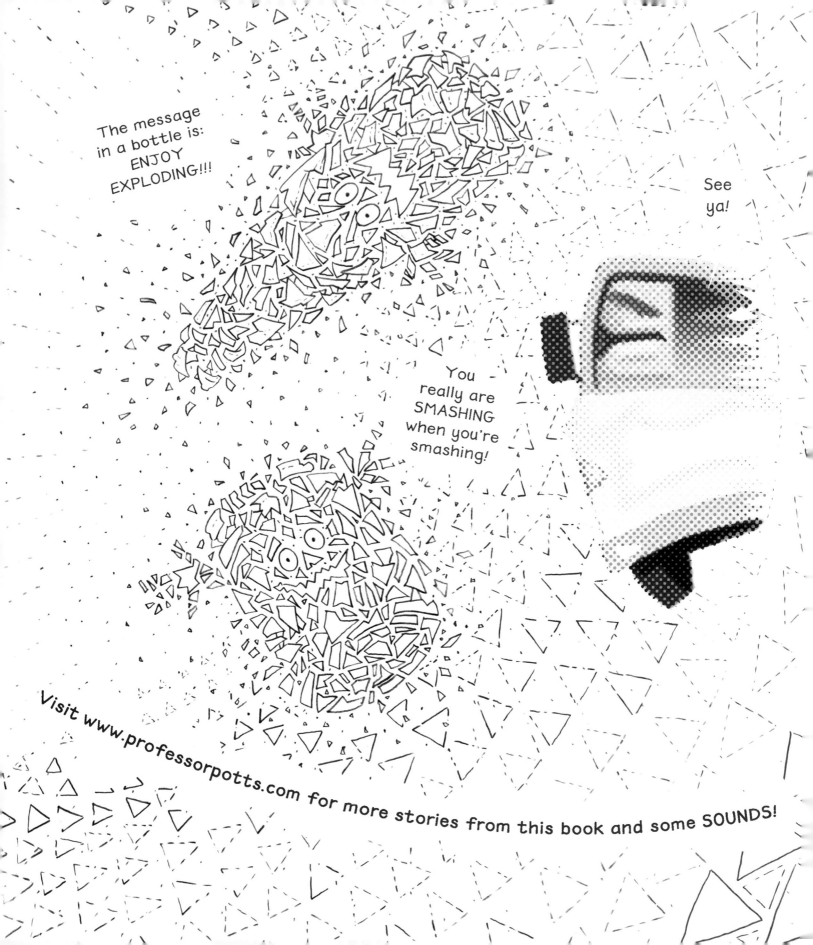

The message in a bottle is: ENJOY EXPLODING!!!

See ya!

You really are SMASHING when you're smashing!

Visit www.professorpotts.com for more stories from this book and some SOUNDS!